"Everyone already knows Lee Tonouchi is funny. *Moments in da Life of Oriental Faddah and Son* will not disappoint. It is funny. But it also reminds that funny is the straight line made vulnerable. And as you are there laughing, this book keeps hitting you in the gut with its vulnerability, with its sentiment of care."

Juliana Spahr
co-editor, *Chain*

"Lee Tonouchi is an expert writer in the language of pidgin. Even more, he champions the language like no one else. Lee is simply among the best poets in the language—one of our irreplaceable treasures. Read him and see."

Frank Stewart
co-editor, *Voices from Okinawa*

"Lee Tonouchi documents several aspects of the history of Uchinānchu in 20th c. Hawai'i as he shares intimate, significant moments in the life of one Local Okinawan family. And, he shares these moments with well-modulated eloquence—sometimes evoking laughter; other times, tears. His words will compel you to move your lips and you will find yourself reading aloud—reveling in pidgin, the connective tissue that keeps us together in Hawai'i."

Michiko Kodama-Nishimoto
lead researcher/interviewer, *Uchinanchu*

"Language issues are at the forefront of this semi-autobiographical sequence of poems, by turns comical and tragic. When the poet tells his Pidgin-speaking grandfather "he should write down all his recipes / so he no forget 'em," he's told: "No can depend book. / In case lose, wot? / Mo' bettah leave in head / den stay inside / forevah." The poet's grandmother, asked to help her grandson with his Japanese homework, teaches him Okinawan Pidgin instead (and he wonders why his grades are falling). Grandma worries about family names, what they really mean. The college girlfriend corrects him when he calls his silent father "Oriental." Fortunately for his readers, Da Pidgin Guerrilla does not always listen to his elders, or his girlfriends. These poems come to us from the outside, but no can forget 'em."

Susan M. Schultz
editor, *Tinfish*

"Through the uniqueness of language, humor, and lore, we go on a journey from youth to adulthood, learning about Hawai'i and Okinawan cultures. Memorable family members people this poet's story. Lee A. Tonouchi plays with both stereotypes and the politically correct in the search for identity."

Alice E. Rogoff
co-editor, *Haight Ashbury Literary Journal*

"Lee Tonouchi wan maesta kraefta. fo dis buk had fo tel wat fo ril aen wat mek biliv, bat hi tek as go holoholo spak enekain in hiz laif. hi tawk abaut hau wi ste luzin da we liv. aez ril dip daet! evretaim ai riD om, ai krai insai. sheim yae bat, go krai in pablik, so ai hol om baek insai an ai jas tek da buk wit mi go benjo aen bakalus krai mai aiz aut. pathos—ai tingk aes da klouses in English fo diskraib wat da buk get."

Kent "Yoda" Sakoda
co-author, *Pidgin Grammar: An Introduction to the Creole Language of Hawai'i*

Significant Moments in da Life of
Oriental Faddah and Son:
One Hawai'i Okinawan Journal

Lee A. Tonouchi

3565 Harding Avenue, Honolulu, Hawai'i 96816
www.BessPress.com

Copyright © 2011 by Bess Press, Inc.

ALL RIGHTS RESERVED

No part of this book may be reproduced or transmitted in
any form by any means, electronic or mechanical, including*
photocopying and recording, or by any information storage
or retrieval system, without permission in writing from the
copyright holder.

Proofreader: Normie Salvador
Okinawan Proofreader: Grant "Sandaa" Murata

Library of Congress Cataloging-in-Publication Data

Tonouchi, Lee A.
   Significant moments in da life of Oriental faddah and
son : one Hawaiʻi Okinawan journal / Lee A. Tonouchi.
      p. cm.
   ISBN-13: 978-1-57306-334-0
   ISBN-10: 1-57306-334-7
   1. Japanese Americans—Hawaii—Biography. 2. Pidgin
English—Hawaii—Texts.   I. Title.
PS571.H3 T66 2011
996.9`092—dc22

                                    2011940263

Cover design by Mariko Merritt

Dis book stay dedicated to my Faddah,
Clarence N. Tonouchi, 1941-2011.

Note

Dis collection of poetry stay semi-autobiographicals. Sometimes names wuz changed and people and situations wuz composited. Couple few tings is entirely made up too. Generally, my feeling is dat it's more funner for da reader if I no reveal which parts is fictions. Da only one I going tell is I nevah go UC Irvine (not dat get anyting wrong wit dat school). Shoooots.

Table of Contents

Acknowledgements

The Asian Pacific American Journal: "Da Art of Eating,"
"Grandpa's Ancient Medicine"

Bamboo Ridge: Journal of Hawai'i Literature and Arts:
"Apart of History," "Wot is Banzai?"

boundary 2: an international journal of literature and culture:
"Diff'rent Stations"

Brooklyn Review: "For da Funeral"

Chain: "Grandpa's Ancient Medicine"

Chaminade Literary Review: "Brainstorm: How Fo' Be Mo'
Okinawan," "Kaimukī Grandma on Being Uchinānchu," "Mazinga Z"

*Coloring Book: An Eclectic Anthology of Fiction and Poetry
by Multicultural Writers:* "All Mix Up"

580 Split: "Da Secret Origin of Oriental Faddah"

Haight Ashbury Literary Journal: "Career Day,"
"Da River Street Gambler"

The Hawai'i Herald: "Hod Work"

The Hawai'i Review: "Cleansing"

Hawai'i Pacific Review: "Da Fort Street Musician"

The Honolulu Star-Bulletin: "Wot Village You From?"

Honolulu Stories: Voices of the Town Through the Years:
"Wot Village You From?"

Kaimana: "Culture Day,"
"Why I Hate Teachers Who Nevah Seen Star Wars"

The Literary Review: "Bridge Building," "No Escape"

Making Lava: "Dear Kikaida"

The Meridian Anthology of Contemporary Poetry:
"Da Photo Album My Mom Made"

New Writing: "Maui Grandma's Regret," "Whole Pig We Eat"

The New York Quarterly (forthcoming):
"Da Day I Forgot my Oriental Faddah had Polio"

The North American Review: "Wot Bruce Lee Sed to Me,"
"Wot School You Went?"

Prism International: "Choosing one Cat"

Rattle: "Batteries," "I Wuz Dea"

Red Shoe: "Significant Moments in da Life of Oriental Faddah and
Son: BIRTH, PUBERTY, COLLEGE, MARRIAGE, DEATH"

Thymos Anthology of Asian American Writing (forthcoming):
"Obaban's Hands," "Significant Moments in da Life of Oriental
Faddah and Son: BIRTH, PUBERTY, COLLEGE, MARRIAGE,
DEATH"

Tinfish: "Wot Village You From?"

Lee A. Tonouchi—Guerrilla Poet

Who Da Guy? He "Da Word" Warrior

Lee A. Tonouchi's *Significant Moments in da Life of Oriental Faddah and Son: One Hawaiʻi Okinawan Journal* is a first-of-its-kind poetry collection that uniquely features a Pidgin, Local Hawaiʻi, Okinawan American narrator. Tonouchi's work is an honest exploration of a range of powerful themes. Some of the themes deal with specific inter-personal relationships like: father-son, especially between Asian Americans males; a child growing up dealing with the death of a parent; and the interaction between a child and his immigrant grandparents. Some themes have resonance with a broader scope such as the generational memories of migration and diaspora for Okinawans who landed in Hawaiʻi, and identity formation for the post-migration generations who straddle multiple cultural boundaries and who experienced successive layers of marginalization. Other themes explore the dynamics of power relations between kids and adults, between men and women, between Local Okinawans and Local Japanese, and between Locals and outsiders.

What this collection has in common with all of Tonouchi's works is the author's unwavering commitment to the goals of his mission to change the deep-seated negative misconception about Hawaiʻi Creole (or HC, locally known as Pidgin with a capital P, as opposed to the linguistic term pidgin with a lower case p) that it is a deformed, bastardized version of English that arose because Locals are too stupid and too lazy to learn English.

The origins of Pidgin date back to the mid-1800s when as a result of Hawaiʻi's socio-economic history of capitalist colonization via the sugarcane and pineapple industries that led to the use of imported labor from among diverse linguistic areas such as China, Portugal, Japan, Okinawa, Puerto Rico, Korea, and the Philippines, Pidgin emerged as a language of expedience for commerce. The word pidgin itself is said to have been derived from a pronunciation of a Cantonese word for 'business'. Contrary to the widely held misperception that Pidgin is a defective or bastardized version of English, or to the larger misconception that it even is an English, it is in fact an intertwined language resulting from years of contact between Hawaiian and English, with English serving as the superstrate language shaping the external features of Pidgin and Hawaiian serving as the substrate language underlying Pidgin's grammatical base. Each in its time and each in its way, contributing languages such as English, Hawaiian, Japanese, Portuguese, Cantonese and others have added vocabulary, idioms, and other grammatical features to what was already a unique hybrid. The first speakers of Hawaiʻi's pidgin were native speakers of their own mother tongues, all the while creating the newly emerging pidgin language as a second language for communication with peoples across cultures in the same adopted island chain. As a living language, Pidgin has moved beyond its initial stage as a linguistic pidgin (arising from three or more mutually exclusive languages) to a subsequent-descendant creole whereby a generation of children end up speaking Pidgin as their first or native language: hence the current more linguistically accurate label of Hawaiʻi Creole. At present there are probably no surviving speakers of that original first Hawaiʻi born pidgin—today all speakers of Pidgin are actually speakers of Hawaiʻi Creole, a true endemic language.

Tonouchi considers his greatest challenge to be changing the way people perceive HC—not only people in positions of institutional power, but surprisingly, the Local Hawaiʻi speakers of HC themselves as well. These are the very people who have been conditioned to believe the negative stereotypes about HC and its speakers. Tonouchi wants the world to acknowledge that HC is a living language capable of conveying serious and complex thought and that it possesses its own linguistic and literary history which deserves to be embraced, valued, documented, and celebrated. With his campaign to raise awareness and pride in being an HC speaker, Tonouchi is consciously striving to break others free from this process of internalized discrimination, with Locals seeing themselves and their own culture through the negative lens of their colonizers. This is exactly what Kenyan academic and activist Ngũgĩ wa Thiong'o argues in *Decolonising the Mind: The Politics of Language in African Literature* (1986), a pivotal work laying the groundwork for post-colonial theory.

Although dubbed "Da Pidgin Guerrilla," Tonouchi takes a very different approach from Ngũgĩ wa Thiong'o. Tonouchi's tactics have a distinctly Local sensibility, an implicit understanding that overly direct, aggressive campaigns are doomed to fail in Hawai'i. His most effective weapon in his arsenal is polished, economical style laced with humor. Humor functions as a conflict-diffuser, an equalizer, and the lubricant with which to very stealthily slide in his ideological arguments about power relations embedded in language. His method is simple. He bombards the public with high-quality, highly visible projects that demonstrate over and over again the way HC can multi-task: it can be funny, serious, and smart at the same time. He sneakily wins his audiences over not by the blunt force of dogma, but disarmingly through buss-laugh or gut-busting humor. He reveals the incongruities created by linguistic power imbalances between Pidgin and English in everyday situations, and skillfully elicits from his audiences a willingness to see a totally different perspective they may not have previously considered.

Oriental, Local Okinawan, and Proud of It

Two key words—Oriental and Okinawan—in Tonouchi's *Significant Moments in da Life of Oriental Faddah and Son: One Hawai'i Okinawan Journal*, provide an historical and sociological context for the collection. The use of the term 'Oriental' denotes that this work, reflecting the Local Asian experience in Hawai'i, is unique from the usual trajectory of Asian American identity formation in the continental United States. In the wake of Edward Said's groundbreaking post-colonial theories published in *Orientalism* (1978), it was finally articulated that the imperialist agenda of

Occidental studies of the Orient is to deem that all things different from the status quo is by default inferior and subordinate. The term 'Oriental' thereafter has been marked as a derogatory racial term. U. S. continental Asian Americans are dutifully instructed to never identify themselves as an 'Oriental' as it would signify acquiescence and collusion with an inherently racist, imperialist value system. However, given Hawai'i's specific racial history resulting in a majority population of non-white Americans, the term 'Oriental' was appropriated by the various assimilated Asian immigrant groups themselves to refer to themselves. As an act of self-naming and re-appropriation of an identity, the use of the term 'Oriental' has a very different connotation in Hawai'i than it does on the North American continent. For many Locals in Hawai'i, 'Oriental' is an identity that is embraced. Taken at face value, 'Oriental' appears to objectively and neutrally describe the region of the Asian continent where some Local people emigrated from.

That said, the use of 'Oriental' in Hawai'i does not mean that racial discrimination against Local, non-white Americans did not exist. It occurred and continues to surface in numerous ways both overt and subtle, as Tonouchi's characters of the narrator, Oriental Faddah and Maui Grandma and Grandpa both encounter and come to terms with it in the following poems: all five title poems under the heading "Significant Moments in the Life of Oriental Faddah and Son": "Birth," "Puberty," "College," "Marriage," and "Death"; "Maui Grandma's Regret," "Apart of History," "Getting One Date for Prom," "Da Secret Origin of Oriental Faddah," "Diff'rent Stations," "All Mix Up," and "Grandpa's Ancient Medicine." As an example, in "Maui Grandma's Regret," Maui Grandma speaks of her only regret that she succumbed to the pressure to rely on Western medical doctors to treat her son's polio through surgery. She wonders what might of happened had her son continued with the Local Japanese yaito (moxibustion) treatment. In "Apart of History," the narrator's uncle reveals how his fellow soldiers forced him to pose as a dead body of a defeated Viet Cong for souvenir photographs to send home.

The second key term—Okinawan—in the collection's title

provides insight into another unique perspective. The American reading audience is familiar with the stories of immigrants arriving in the United States from China, Japan, Korea, Vietnam, Laos, and the Philippines; but the trajectory of Okinawan immigrants is less widely known because their stories have been subsumed by the more widely known Japanese American experience of war and internment and reintegration into American society. Although Okinawan immigrants to America were often mistaken for Japanese and shared the same fate as Japanese immigrants in the U.S. during WWII, Okinawans have their own culture and history, distinct from Japan's. Tonouchi's collection, by the same token, offers a narrative perspective that is divergent from those of the Local Japanese experience in Hawai'i. While Tonouchi expresses a Local Okinawan perspective, it is important to distinguish the identity that his poems represent with the larger historical context of what it means to be Okinawan.

To clarify, three terms are used to describe this group of people: Ryukyuan, Uchinānchu, and Okinawan. Ryūkyū is the name for the geographic group of islands between Kyūshū island of Japan and Taiwan; it also describes the indigenous peoples who inhabit this island group (people from each of the following islands or island regions: Amami, Okinawa, Miyako, Yaeyama and Yonaguni); and finally, it is the name used to describe the independent sovereign kingdom that governed the indigenous peoples of this region between 1429 and 1879. The Ryūkyū Kingdom maintained a tributary relationship to China and Japan until it was invaded and annexed by Japan in 1879. It was occupied by the U.S. in the aftermath of WWII in 1945 and eventually remanded back to Japan in 1972.

Uchinānchu is the indigenous name of the Okinawan culture, island, and people that is used by Okinawans to refer to themselves to distinguish themselves from the Naichi (mainland) Japanese. Uchināguchi is the term used for one of the languages in the Ryukyuan language group that is spoken on Okinawa and is a distinct and separate language from Japanese. It is not to be confused with Okinawan Japanese (Uchinā yamatoguchi), which is Japanese spoken with an Okinawan accent. The increase in the use of the term Uchinānchu represents a growing self-determination as evidenced by the proliferation of Okinawan studies by Okinawans themselves.

Okinawa is the name of the language and culture of a specific island in the Ryūkyū Island group, and it is also the name of the Japanese prefecture that covers all of the Ryūkyū Islands. It is this last fact that accounts for why most of the specificity of the Ryukyuan diverse cultures, languages, and history is not so widely known outside of the Ryūkyūs and Japan, such as in the United States, due to the fact that all of that area is identified under a single prefecture name—Okinawa.

When most American readers encounter Okinawan, the word actually refers to the Ryukyuans who emigrated away from their archipelago, even though not all immigrants from this region come from the island of Okinawa. Influenced by the American Civil Rights movement of the 1960s-1970s, subsequent generations descended from Ryukyuan immigrants to America (known as Okinawan Americans) began to assert their own identity separate from that of the Japanese Americans.

The Okinawan experience that Tonouchi's collection seeks to articulate is specifically fourth-generation Okinawan American, growing up in Hawaiʻi in the 1970s and beyond. So the Local Hawaiʻi Okinawans are to be distinguished from Ryukyuan Okinawans and the Local Japanese in Hawaiʻi. The poems that address the Local Hawaiʻi Okinawan identity are: "Why I Hate Teachers Who Nevah Seen Star Wars," "Whole Pig We Eat," "Culture Day," " 'Wot Village You From?' " "Wot Village I From," "All Mix Up," "Wot is Banzai?" "Wot School You Went," "Obaban's Hands," "Hajichi: Tattoos and Diamonds is Forevah," "Palms Face Up," "Brainstorm: How Fo' Be Mo' Okinawan," "Kaimukī Grandma On Being Uchinānchu," "How I Post to Know?" "Naming One Okinawan Baby," "Okinawan Proverb," "Da Fort Street Musician," "Chiburu Journal," and "Grandma's Boxes."

So What's It About?
A Boy and His Life of Multiple Marginalizations

What makes this collection of poems compelling is the surprising multi-dimensional depth that belies its understated simplicity. On the surface, it is the story of a young man coming to terms with his mother's death when he was a child; and of the evolving relationship with his father and grandparents in the aftermath of that inexplicable tragedy.

What complicates this exploration of personal identity is the multiple layers of marginalization that the narrator experiences. He grows up as a Pidgin speaker in a place where English is the dominant language of ostensible economic, social and political power ("Hod Work"). He grows up marginalized as Local in Hawai'i when all of the mainstream portrayals of adolescence are white continental Americans ("Diff'rent Stations," "Apart of History"). He grows up marginalized as an American in Hawai'i where the ghosts of his parents' and grandparents' ethnic history and identity continue to challenge his sense of who he is ("Whole Pig We Eat," "Obaban's Hands," "Hajichi: Tattoos and Diamonds is Forevah," "Palms Facing Up," "Naming One Okinawan Baby"). He grows up marginalized as a Local Okinawan in a place dominated by the Local Japanese, where discriminatory attitudes of Japan Nationals towards Okinawans, the subjugated second-class citizens of Japan, are replicated in Hawai'i ("Why I Hate Teachers Who Nevah Seen Star Wars," "Culture Day," "Career Day," "Kaimukī Grandma On Being Uchinānchu,"). And he grows up marginalized as a Local Okinawan American as opposed to the Okinawans who stayed in the motherland and did not emigrate ("Da Fort Street Musician," "Brainstorm: How Fo' Be Mo' Okinawan," "Chiburu Journal").

With each poem, the reader digs a little deeper into the questions that the narrator explores: Who am I? How am I different from my friends at school? Why am I being picked on for being hairy? How come Grandma talks funny? How come Grandma knows so much about how to cook and eat a pig? Why does Grandma take pictures with her gloves on? How come no one really wants to listen and learn from Grandma? What did Grandma think about Dad when he had polio growing up? How did my parents choose each other and fall in love? Why is Dad so uncommunicative verbally? Doesn't Dad miss Mom as much as I do? Why are Okinawans not the same as Japanese? Why did I throw away so many opportunities to learn from Grandma and Dad before it was too late?

Da Take Away

A truly skillful poet is someone who is able to seamlessly transport you into another person's life so unlike your own, make you actually care about who that person is and what that person is going through, and then bring you back to yourself barely cognizant of the journey you have just completed—because all of what you have just lived through while reading becomes in a very real way an intimate and integral part of your own experience. Other hallmarks of a skilled poet are: first, mindful modulation of perspective, inflection, and rhythm; and second, the carefully honed artistry of internal poetic architecture, word choice and irony to reflect a multiplicity and depth of meanings. All of these are on display in this collection of poems written in Tonouchi's characteristically low-key and humble Local Pidgin style.

In *Significant Moments in da Life of Oriental Faddah and Son: One Hawai'i Okinawan Journal*, Tonouchi is able to intricately weave together his pitch-perfect Local Pidgin voice, his finely-tuned Local Comedic timing and subtly nuanced flashes of irony, to create the narrative persona of a fourth-generation Local Okinawan in Hawai'i seeking to define himself within the context of his relationships with his mother, father, grandmother, grandfather, and girlfriend and future-wife. So vivid are the characters you meet, the voices from the different generations that you hear, and the wide array of emotions that you experience vicariously, that as you read the entire collection from beginning to end as a single unified entity, you are left with the very strong impression that you have just finished reading a novel spanning the life of a Local Oriental father through the eyes of his son.

The deceptive thing about this collection of poems is that it makes no grand claims to represent the Okinawan experience. However, Tonouchi introduces a particular poetic narrative voice that has not yet been seen in Local Literature or Pidgin Literature— exploring what it means to be human through the eyes of a Local Hawaiʻi Okinawan American young man growing up in the 1970s. Overall, there is pleasure in simply reading them for the poems they are. Thoughtful, touching, resonant, and well-written, each hits you with a zing! and then doesn't let you go. They stick with you as you walk around for a while in someone else's skin, thinking their thoughts, feeling their pain and joy. Best of all, these poems make you laugh—coming from someplace deep within—as you realize that the brain tickle is spontaneous and spot on.

Micheline M. Soong, Ph.D.
Associate Professor, Department of English
Hawaiʻi Pacific University

Significant Moments in da Life of Oriental Faddah and Son: BIRTH

I would like fo' tink
he started off wit one
yosh.

Or, if he wuz feeling
particularly peppy
maybe one unbridled,
one unrestrained
YOOOOOOOOOOOOOSH
for demonstrate
his virility.

Cuz I know
my Oriental Faddah,
he not one man
of many words,
of much emotion.
He probably made due wit
grunt.

Jus one grunt
fo' send da message
he done,
through,
all pau,
time fo' go sleep now.

Das all I can imagine
my Oriental Faddah saying
when him and my Ma
wuz trying for conceive me.

He jus not da type fo' say
"Oh yeah,
work it, baby, work it.
C'mon down,
let's get funky
like a monkey."

Nope.
Grunt.
Jus one.

Maui Grandma's Regret

You tink
you Faddah born la'dat, HAH?!
Him husky boy was, you know.
Him and Alvin allatime
go play down da ditch.

One day big rain
you Faddah catch fever,
body come numb.
We all some worry.
Da doctor, nurse
no like touch you Faddah.
Dey tink contagious, polio.
Nobody like go by him.

Our Bāsan, Jīsan tell
bring him home, bring him home.

Da doctor happy, tell go, go.

We take him drive go see
Toyama Jīsan down Waikapū.
He know
wot everybody dunno.

Everyday he find da point
and he put da herb.
Wit da senkō stick he yaito
and burn you Faddah.
You Faddah no can feel nahting;
his body all stiff.
Neck down

no can move.

Den slow by slow
da nerve come out.
Hand move. Feet move.
Pretty soon can stand up.

But haole lady tell bettah
take 'em go real doctor,
check.

Honolulu Doctor see
he tell, miracle dis boy.

But he say mo' safe
if operate, make shua cure.
Honolulu Doctor make operation
den noddah operation one mo'.
Den put metal brace.

I take you Faddah back Maui.
I opa him, carry him
so he no need limp.

I should've let Toyama Jisan
continue sa'mo was.
Das my only regret.

Batteries

I used to nag my Grandma
buy me toys, buy me toys.
And whenevah she bought me one,
Grandpa would go "Too much omocha."

So raddah than get da scoldings
I used to colleck stuff I found
around da house, like
matchbook covers,
bottlecaps,
used stamps.
I even tried collecking rocks
but wuzn't really
interesting to me.
My Grandpa kept saying I should
colleck leaves.
I tink he wuz trowing da hints like
he wanted me for help him
rake da yard.

Den one day
when I wuz emptying da rubbish can
I found one used battery.
Wuz real diff'rent looking.
Wuz deep blue
and bronze color,
wit one cat drawing on top.
Da shiny metallic colors
wuz pretty trips.

My Mom toll my Dad
abunai,

dangerous if I start
collecking dat kine,
bumbye da acid leak
and might go insai my eye.
God gave us one perfect son
and now this is how we
take care?

I wuz perfeck my Mom sed.
I tot she wuz perfeck too.
I wuz happy God gave her
to me.

My Dad just rolled his eyes
cuz my Mom wuz always worrying about me.
So for make her happy, he toll me
when brown stuff starts for come out
den das when I had for trow 'em away.

Da brown stuff is acid, poison he sed.
But da only time I seen acid come out
wuz when I leff
da flashlight on for like
couple years
and so all da electricity wen go leak.

I figured
so long as
da battery
wuzn't insai anyting
electricals
den nevah need werry.
Safe. Can keep 'em forevah.

One day my Mom took me Shirokiya.

She wuz happy I nevah ask for one toy
in long time
so she sed I can have one
brand new battery,
anyone I wanted.
And Shirokiya had all da
colorful-kine kines from Japan.

Aftah we leff,
My Mom buckled me in my seat
and I put my new green battery
insai my giant nori container.
Me and my Mom wuz
jus driving back home
when all of a sudden
we got bang from da side.
I seen my battery jar
buss open
and all my batteries
wen fly all ova da place.

My Mom wuzn't moving.
She wuzn't checking on me
for see if I wuz okay.
Planny people wuz looking at us
from on top da sidewalk.
And I seen
planny blood leaking
from my Mom.
So much blood
wuz coming out
I knew God wouldn't
let me keep her
anymore.

dear kikaida,

you my favorite japanese
superhero. i watch your tv show
all the time. i seen you at
pearlridge when you come down
but i dont know if you saw me
cause had plenny kids there and
you was kinda busy fighting the
monsters of the dark.

i was wondering maybe next
time when you come hawaii maybe
you can help me out. see cause
i get one problem thats same as
you and almost similar. i know
where my dad stay but i
dunno where my mom went. last
i seen her was in the
ambulance.

my dad said she died. but im thinking
the hospital people never showed me
the body. the dark could be taking
over hawaii and maybe the hospital
is part of their secret base. maybe
my mom just has amnesia now like
your dad dr komyoji. maybe shes lost.
maybe shes wandering around the
other side of the island like in nanakuli.

if you had time when you not busy
saving mitsuko, masaru, and all of
japan. maybe you can try fly around
the island look real fast see if you can
spot my mom someplace, or if my dad
lets i can ride in your motorcycle
sidecar and help you look cause you
might not know what she looks like.

Your ichiban #1 kikaida fan

Choosing one Cat

When Neko Chan died
my Dad took me
Humane Society
but I nevah like get
one noddah cat.

He sed sometimes cats
get re-in-carnationed
and dey come back
in diff'rent bodies
but dat nevah make me
feel bettah
cuz looking at all da cats
had too many;
all of 'em
could've been her.

So I wen ax him,
how I 'post to
recognize?

She used to be
da black and white
sumotori cat
but now
looking at all
da little ones
run around
wot if
she wuz in one diff'rent body?
All kalakoa she could be,
wotchoo call 'em?

Da kine calico cat
or maybe she wuz one
orange Haole cat now.

And wot if she wuzn't even
one cat
or one dog
or anyting dey had
at da Humane Society?

Wot if she wuz
one FLOWER
or someting?

I figgah das why
dey call 'em
re-in-CARNATION, no?

So how I going know?
Flowers not fluffy.
Flowers no make purr purr.
And flowers no can meow

I had so much questions,
so he wen jus change
his mind
about re-in-carnation.

"No mo' such ting," he sed.
"Once you gone,
you gone.
Pau.
Das it.
End of story."

Wot Bruce Lee Sed to Me

In da beginning
of *Enter the Dragon*
Bruce Lee
toll da boy
for fight
wit emotional content,
but not anger.

When da boy did 'em
Bruce wen ax
"How did it feel to you?"
Da boy made da mistake
of saying
"Let
me
think."

Ho, Bruce wen shnap.
"Don't think,
feeeeeel.
It is like a finger pointing
away to the moon.
Don't concentrate
on the finger
or you will miss allll
that heavenly glory."

HAH?, I tot.
Wotchoo talking?

But den wuz like
at least Bruce toll 'em

someting.
I imagined maybe
insai
dat message,
maybe had someting
intended
for me.

Cuz aftah my Mom
passed away
my Faddah nevah
try explain
to me,
da reasonings.

But oddah people,
stranger people even,
dey always sed stuff like
"Everyting happens
for a reason."
"Don't worry,
she's in a better place now."
Or "God always takes
the good ones first,"
in which case I tot
wot's da sense
in being good den?

J'like da young waitress
at da restaurant
who always seen
me and my Faddah,
jus us two,
come in for eat all da time,

so one day
she finally asks me
"Where's your Mommy?"
not knowing
wot she wuz getting
herself into
by asking
such one deep
question.

Mazinga Z

My Dad used to take me movies
everytime he had off.
We used to go Empress
in Chinatown for check out
da latest kung-fu movies.
Sometimes we used to go
Kaimukī Theater matinee
cuz had *Mazinga Z*, li'dat.

I really wanted dat Mazinga toy
da one in da case at Shirokiya.
I nevah like ax my Dad
cuz he jus wen spend
ukubillion dollars on my glasses.
I tot wuz goofy looking,
but he sed at least I can
read da sub-titles when we go movies.

One time he had to work extra
so I toll Grandma I wanted fo' walk
up da street by myself.
She sed be careful and she gave me money.
I remembah dat day had
one big Mazinga statue outside.
Ho, da buggah wuz humangous,
but I guess wen only look big to me
cuz I wuz only one little kid.
I wuz mo' old than da cut-off age,
but I figgah-ed I could still get in
at da cheaper rate.
I nevah like pay da full ting,
cuz I wanted fo' save some

for snack maybe.

When I went fo' buy my ticket
I took off my glasses.
Dat way da ticket man's face
look all blurry ah.
I figgah if I wuz looking at him
eye to eye
would've been hod fo' lie
if he wen ax me how old I wuz.
All fo' nothin' wuz
cuz da old ticket man
nevah even ax fo' I.D.
But I guess he wen trust me
cuz I had one on-ess face.

I forget who da bad guy wuz dat day
but I tink wuz da one wea
Doctor Demon stole da Super Alloy Z.
I jus remembah I had hod time paying attention.
Everytime da usher came in
I kept lookin'
lookin' over my shoulder.
I kept tinking if dey wuz going find me.
Maybe I should've sat
mo' in da middle.

When I got home
my Dad finally came
so he axed me how wuz.
I told him wuz okay.
He told me he jus got one raise
so he took me down Shirokiya
and said I could have
any one toy.

I jus chose one plastic Ultra 7 monster.
I nevah even look wot had
insai da glass case.

Why I Hate Teachers Who Nevah Seen *Star Wars*

I wear long pants,
long sleeve shirt,
but too late
everybody in school
already seen da shame
I trying for hide.

Aftah *Star Wars* comes out
all da kids start calling me
CHEWBACCA,
cuz I full Okinawan,
so outta everybody
in da school
I get da hairiest arms,
da hairiest legs,
and da hairiest head.
And even though I no mo' hair
on my face
I guess to dem das
close enough related
dat apparently I can pass
for being
one WOOKIE.

Bad enough da teacher,
her, she no even notice
all da red dots on my arms,
da puka patches of skin
on top my limbs
for wea all my fur
used to be.

Da worstest is when
da teacher helps dem,
by supplying 'em
wit da invisible weapon
dey need
for turn me
into one human ripper wallet.

"Mrs. Oshio, you get Scotch tape?"
dey ask.
And she GEEVS 'em.
And not jus one piece.
Da WHOLE ROLL.

And when she ask wot da tape for,
dey say we jus playing *Star Wars*.
She no catch on
when dey tell
I playing da role of Chewbacca
and I going be
their prisoner.

Whole Pig We Eat

Bāsan raise da pig wuz.
Some, da small one, she sell.
When da pig ready,
wit da knife
she poke da neck,
kill 'em, take da blood out
and da pig ma-ke.
Bāsan make big pot full
of water.
She boil, boil, boil 'em,
den everybody come over
and pour da hot water ova da pig
and dey scrape wit da knife,
take da hair off,
clean 'em, and den wash.
She call Jīsan.
Jīsan cut da head off
and cut da stomach now,
from up straight go cut da stomach
and den she take all da inside out,
all hemo.

Next one, Bāsan clean da intestine.
Oh, das da big job.
Not one person can do it.
Two, tree person come
and take all da intestine,
inside no one
dey take it all off
and den wash 'em
and den turn 'em insai out,
and den dey soap 'em in da soap.

Bāsan cook wit da soap,
den clean wit da water.
Aftah all pau,
she mix wit da cooking oil aru no ga.
Cook long time da intestine,
cook wit da pork
and you eat it.

Da stomach Bāsan clean,
cook in da water long time,
till da stomach come soft.
Aftah dat Bāsan cook wit da meat,
make soup outta dat.
She take da pig blood,
dey leave 'em little while in da pot
and da pig blood going get hard see,
den she cook da pig blood separate.
When da pork is cook,
she cut da pig blood,
slice yo, den cook togeddah. Eat.

Da liver separate.
Bāsan boil it, slice it,
and serve wit da salt.
Okinawa style, liver is very
important.
New Year day dey haff to have
for decoration
for ageru kine. When dey offer
dey haff to have liver,
offer for prayer.
Aftah you prayer den you eat it.
Everybody going eat.
Taste ono.

Heart, all da organ can eat.
Even tail. Scrape 'em off,
cut 'em and can eat.
Eye eat. Tongue too no can waste.
Da ear da good one.
We all fight for da ear.
Too bad all dat kine
you nevah eat before.
Dey no sell 'em in da store as why
so you young folks dunno, yeah?

Da feet too, you clean 'em good, add kobu,
da green one, cook long time.
You haff to take da toenail out, you know?
Godda clean 'em good.
Scrape 'em, scrape 'em.
Not easy job make pig feet soup.

Okinawa smart use pig.

Pig head good make da medicine.
For da headache.
Grandpa everytime used to get sore head.
Bāsan clean da pig head
and make soup wit dat.
Old people, dey make medicine,
wit da head aru ga.
I dunno wot dey used to put,
das da one main ting.
Das why no sense telling.
I dunno wot Bāsan used to put.
Somekine leaf, herb,
she add da ingredients
den tied 'em all up wit da skin
and steam 'em long time.

In da bone, get da inside one.
From dat one da gravy going come down,
das da medicine.
Grandpa drink da shinji.
Den headache pau, gone.

When Bāsan make dat time
I no watch.
Lazy me wuz.
I tink bumbye I going haff to help.
But now I wish I knew
all da one she put insai.
Really good medicine dat.
Pohō I no learn wuz.
Pohō.

Culture Day

Teacher like us present
one food from our cultural group
and bring 'em to class
for share wit everybody
on Culture Day.

Grandma sez
Okinawans get andāgī,
but too dangerous teach me make
cuz da oil hot, abunai.
Bumbye da oil fly
and I might get burn.

Maui Grandma tells me
how Okinawans
is famous
for pig.
But all da pig part dishes
dey used to make, I tink
is kinda gross.

I like get one good grade,
and since my cooking abilities
is limited
to foods I
can microwave,
I decide for chop up
some Spam.

I cut 'em in cubes
and nuke 'em on high.
When pau, aftah da ting die,

I trow one toothpick
in each one,
for make
little bit fancy,
for add
dat little bit
of extra class.

I figgah
Teacher going love
my Spam pupus
cuz it's like instead
of all da pig organs
being in separate dishes,
everyting all stay
in one dish.
It's like eating twelve
Okinawan dishes
all one time.

Without going into
too many embarassing details
I jus give my speech
about how Okinawans love pig.
And how Spam
get allllll da pig components
dat Okinawans love best.
So in a way I say
my Spam pupus
is actually. . .
SUPER
Okinawan.

But from da grade I get
I can tell

Teacher must not be into
da kine MODERN
Okinawan cuisine.

Career Day

I all excited.
Today is career day
when everybody gotta go up in front da class
and talk fass kine
about wot kine job their dads get.

One by one, everybody goes up.

Kathy's dad is one biologist.
David's dad works for da City and County.
Doris's dad works for da newspapah.

Everybody's dad is so BORING.
I cannot wait
for tell da class wot mines one does.
Going blow da doors off Kent's dad.
I dunno why he making big deal
his faddah own gas station.
Not like any of us can drive.

When my turn comes
I look at da class,
den I look at Mrs. Nakasone.
She nods her head at me
giving me da signal, like goin' goin'.

I guess I little bit nervous
cuz I dunno my arms is flapping
back and forth
until Mrs. Nakasone
asks me if I preparing for lift-off.
So I'm all like "Hah?"

And by da time I catch on
she all impatient already,
"Tell the class
what your father does for a living."

Oh yeah yeah yeah.
K, you ready?
He work Ka'ena Point.
You know wea's dat, ah?
Das like supa far away
at da end of da island.
I know you tinking das like booney land,
how anybody can work ova dea.
I know cuz das wot I wuz tinking too.
Same same brah, da way our minds work.
But I found out, he works for da government.
Da United States Air Force fo' be exack.
It's called da Hawai'i Tracking Station,
but no tell nobody
cuz da name is secret.
When dey answer da phone, dey gotta tell
da special CODE name, Hula.
Hello, Hula. Who dis?
Hula no stand for nahting;
I know cuz I asked.
It's jus Hula,
like I found out
Kody is da nickname
for Alaska or wotevahs.
Planny of da work he does
is all top secret kine stuff
so he cannot talk about 'em.
But I toll 'em I needed some
specifics for my report
so he toll me dey responsible

for tracking satellites and stuff
from all da way out
in outer space.
Chi-haw! How's dat?!

I take my bow
and wait for everybody clap.
But nobody does.

I hear Randall Wakumoto whisper
to da girls in da corner, "Das so shibai."
Da girls start giggling.
Den Kent adds "Yeah, bull lie, brah.
I bet his faddah really one teacher,
or someting boring li'dat.
Oh, no offense, Mrs. Nakasone."

I look down and I notice
my arms all flapping again,
so I slow 'em down gradual
and I put my wings
back in check.
Cuz from dea
wea else can I go
except
back to my seat?

Lee Tonouchi
Period 4
Social Studies
Jan. 31, 1983

D+

A part Of History

I asked my dad if we had anybody in our family from World War I, World War II, or maybe the Civil War. I don't know why he laughed before answering, but he told me Uncle Al, the Uncle with the beard, the one who smokes and drinks plenty beer, he went Vietnam to be a helicopter mechanic.

I called up Uncle Al and asked him if what my dad said was real life true story. He wanted to know why I wanted to know, so I told him it was for school and the teacher wanted us to start doing research and find out if we had anybody in our family that was a part of history. Then I asked him if he got shot plenty times, if his friends died over there, if he was scared he wasn't ever gonna come back home.

He said "Yeah" to all these questions so I asked him to share with me one of the stories. He said, "The guys from my platoon went go ask me for lie down on top the ground, stick out my tongue, and make actor, while they went go step my chest and point the gun down at my forehead. All that just so they could take picture, send home for souvenir.

Did you make this up!? I've never read anything about this happening before.

"So, did you step on anybody too?" I asked. He said, "No. To the haoles from the mainland, Viet Cong, Locals. We all look same to dem. Till today, I still remember."

That's when my Uncle sounded kinda sad so I told him thanks. I told him I'd call him back later if I had to ask him more questions, and I'd show him my paper when my teacher gave me an "A" for it. Right, Mrs. C?

Next time, it would be preferred if you got your information from the library just so we can be sure.

Da River Street Gambler

I can't believe he
wuz one a-dem
one of their gang,
a band of undah-handed,
unscru-pu-lous
law abusers.

Would I be considered one accessory?
Aftah all, I wuz involve.
I wuz in charge of da loot.
Under-age accomplice
to my Grandpa, also known as
da River Street Gambler.

My Grandma would be all shock
if she knew wea we wuz,
playing Paiyut in public
wea any flat foot patroling da area
could arress us and send us jail.

I wish these guys wouldn't make such a racket
and draw attention to themselves.
Such brazen criminals.

At least dey could play wit bills
cuz if we had to hide da coins fass
would make so much noise.

My Grandpa kept licking his thumb
before drawing one card.
I tot dat wuz kinda gross
'cause his hands wuz always touching money, ah.

But thinking back, maybe
dat wuz for erase da finger prints.
My Grandpa wuz one clever crook.

Maybe I should turn all these guys in.
Maybe my Grandpa can get off if he testifies.
Maybe get one reward
for their capture.

Ees not like me and my Grandpa won big.
I no tink wuz worth da risk.
But aftah da game, my Grandpa took me
around da corner to Chiyo's
and bought me one ice cream cone.

Da police never pieced together da puzzle
of da mysterious identity
of da River Street Gambler.
And my Grandma nevah guessed
I had ice cream.
I licked my fingers clean.

Wot is Banzai?

You Obaban
88 birthday
Tōkachi
special celebration.
Everybody come wuz
eat someting
fo' good luck and long life.
You Ojiji say go let you
Uncle Richard tell da
banzai.

Not anybody can tell you know
only relative or good friend.
Me proud Richard.
When time come
everybody stand up
Richard yell
"Shindo shimpū. . . Banzai!"
Everybody look puzzle.

You Uncle
he should ax befo' wuz.
When you go
make sure you know.
Shinrō shinpū mean
to da bride and groom.

Tōkachi yūwē. . . Banzai.

Significant Moments in da Life of Oriental Faddah and Son: PUBERTY

For my 13th birthday
my Oriental Faddah
gave me my long awaited
Cosby Show talk
about da birds
and da bees.

I know if Da Cos
did 'em
would probably take
forevah and a day
cuz whenevah Da Cos talks
ees always
so drawn out:

"Son, a long time agooooooo
the birds and the beeeeeeeees
hooked up. So that is whyyyyyy
The stork
took over
for them. . ."

I know my Oriental Faddah
could nevah
sustain one speech
fo' dat long.
So I wuz anticipating
someting li'lo bit mo' concise,
but not someting dat would take
only 2.2 seconds.

Cuz all he did wuz hand me
one black T&C T-shirt
wit one smiley face
balloon character
and fluorescent
yellow lettahs dat sed
"No Glove,
No Love."

Das it,
no explainations.
Not even one hint
we wuz talking
metaphor.

"Wot Village You From?"

Grandma axes my friends
wit Okinawan last names.
I dunno why,
cuz she always gets
disappointed
when dey tell
Pālolo.

Wot Village I From

Grandma makes me memorize
in case somebody axes
one day, she sez.
Nobody eva does.

Wot School You Went?

I see my uncle guys
talking story at one party
at da tea house.
Dey axing stranger people
"Wot school you went?"
not "Wot village you from?"
like how my Grandma does 'em.

My Uncle guys laugh
when da haole guy
say UNLV.
He dunno he 'post to tell
his high school.

Da follow-up questions dey ax is
"Wot year you grad?" den dey go
"Eh, you know such and such person?"
And amazing,
but half da time
da oddah guy actually know.

I dunno nobody
not from my school.

When we driving home
I ax my Grandma joking kine,
"Grandma, wot school you went?"
I all ready for say
"Eh, you know my Grandpa?"

But she trow me off
when she no follow da pattern.

She say she nevah go school,
only up to seven grade.

She tell,
"I wanted for be teacher was, do.
But no mo' money. So no can.
I had to work
Lucky 7 Inn.
Ten dollah a month,
plus room and board.
Once a month I go back home
give my faddah da payday,
den same day, go back work.
And all dat money
alllll
go back Okinawa."

"Ho, sound like
das one pretty rod deal."
I tell my Grandma,
"Hakum you nevah say uh-uh,
fly dat,
I ain't giving away
my hard earn money to
da village people?!!"

My Grandma jus look at me
and shakes her head.
She tell me in her stern voice,
"NO. No can.
Godda do.
Das how was."

Getting one Date for Prom

Getting one date for prom
is harder than you tink
especially when
you Oriental.

I tired being
Oriental.

Jus for once
I like be
Non-
Oriental.

Das it.
Das wot I like be.

Cuz girls no like
Oriental guys.

Get too many
das why:
Chinese,
Japanese,
Vietnamese,
Korean,
Filipino,
Laotian,
Okinawan.

Even
da kine
Oriental

combo
no really rate—
Japokinawan
Wot's so special
about dat—
get plannnnnnnny.

Das why
one day
I wish I could be
Haole
or Hawaiian.

Cuz das da kine
girls dig.
Den dey can make
cuuuute Hapa-kine babies.

And it's cool
dey tinking
about having childrens
cuz dat means
dey must be tinking about
doing da DA KINE. Chii!

But den,
no mattahs to me
No mo' any action;
nevah going get
any action.

Cuz nobody
like my baby.

Talkin' 'Bout Tracie

Wuz weird
da first time
I ate dinner
Tracie's house;
da family wuz having
all kine intellectual conversations.

My house
nobody talk
at da dinner table.
When he dea, my Oriental Faddah read da papah.
My Grandma dem watch *Abarenbo Shogun*.
I jus chew my food.

Wuz weird
when I caught ride
wit Tracie and da mom.
Dey wuz all interchanging discourse
'bout skool and work, li'dat.

When my Oriental Faddah drive
nobody talk;
we jus gotta listen
to his junk-kine A.M. station.

Ho, when me and Tracie
wen finally hook up
I wuz all proud ah,
so I wanted fo' show off
to him.

I told 'em
"Guess wot?
Tracie and me stay goin' now."

Den one funny ting wen happen.

My Oriental Faddah wen tilt his head
and he wen ax me
"When she born?"

"July 28," I sed.

"She's a Leo,
you one Leo too.
Both you guys goin' like be boss.
You guys not goin' get along."

Maybe das why I no talk to my Oriental Faddah.

Da Secret Origin of Oriental Faddah

She calls her Faddah Stanley.
I tot dat wuz weird.
So I wen ax her,
"Hakum, you no call your Dad, Dad?"

Das when I tot about 'em,
eh, hakum I
no call mines one Dad?

Most of da time nowdays
I jus call 'em
"Aye."
Like
"Aye, you can sign dis papah for school?"
or
"Aye, Da Kine, I need ride go Kāhala Mall."

First name "Aye."
Last name "Da Kine."

I tink when I wuz smaller
I used to call 'em Dad.
I pretty sure I did.
Cuz Daddy sounds girlie.
Pa is too hillbilly.
Pop sounds too 1950's.
And Father is all religious.

"Well, you are one to talk,"
she tells me back.
"You call your Dad, Oriental Father.
So what's the story with that?"

Well, not like I call 'em dat
to his face, I stay tinking.
Only when I talking about him
to somebody else.

"Good question," I reply.
Wot is da secret origin
of Oriental Faddah
and his sidekick
Son?

Wuz probably cuz
Mrs. Lee's class.
She always saying
how us ORIENTAL kids
gotta be more bettah at
expressing ourselves
verbally,
like her favorite student
Jeffery Nugent.
He's da haole guy from da mainland.

Everytime, whenevah she
ax da class someting
and if nobody talk,
she yell at us.
She sez she wen overcome
her "Oriental handicap,"
so wot wuz
wrong wit us?

And even though planny times
Jeffery no say nahting too,
for him, she wen jus assume he
know da answer,

but jus nevah like show off.

I guess
das when it click for me.
Das why
me and my Oriental Faddah no really
have da kine faddah/son talks
like Ward and da Beav.

If he da Oriental Faddah
den by genetics
me, I da Oriental Son
so both-a-us,
two
no can communicate.

We hopeless
jus like Mrs. Lee sez.

Da Day I Forgot my Oriental Faddah had Polio

We wen park da car
den I
went in da mall
down da escalator
stopped at da bottom
turned around,
looked up,
realized he wuzn't dea,
went back up da escalator
to da entrance,
waited,
held da door open for him
followed him down
until we got
to da ground floor
and went insai
Something Special
wea he wen turn to me
and say
"Why?
You shame?
As why you no stay by me?
You shame you faddah get limp?"

I wanted for say
"No.
I proud. I proud of you.
Grandma sez "Most man,
da wife pass away,
dey would go bar,
everynight drink."
Grandma always tells,

"You get good faddah,
you know dat?
He no go out holoholo.
He stay home,
take care
you."

But I wuz all
self-conscious
cuz people
wuz all staring
at me, as I wuz
shaking my head
half crying
before I wuz finally able
for stammer out
one
"I not shame,"
but he wuz already
gone
someplace
insai da store,
so I nevah know
if he heard
wot I sed
or if he only heard
my
hesitation.

Bridge Building

My Oriental Faddah used to like fixing up his '66 Chevelle.
I wuz shmall so I jus used to sit and look-on all fascinated.

250 matchsticks maximum.

I helped him repair all da appliances around da house.
I wuz like da guy who gives da surgeon da scalpel and junk.

Each stick no shorter than ¾".

High school time, me and my friends used to cruise Fun Factory.
My Oriental Faddah stopped helping me wit my homework at Geometry.

Bridge must span at least 13".

But wuz him who wen help me Junior year wit my science project.
Ms. Hart wuz all impress at his idea fo' make 'em one arch.

Da secret was the special quick dry glue.

I nevah go into automotive, carpentry, electronics, or engineering.
On weekends I read books, comics, but mostly I go visit Tracie.

Da bridge held 18 lbs. before it broke.

Hod Work

Young time
you Grandpa
Cahpentah Foreman you know.
State Capitol Building
you Grandpa
build!

Meeting place hod fo' make wuz.
Not square. Ten point.
Honolulu no' mo' surveyah fo' dat.
As why Reed and Martin
from unibersity hire, engineer.
He point. I mahk.
Concrete all pour.

Following week come,
I finish.
He glad.
Lucky ting I get you.
He say dat you know.

See, you Grandpa no go skool, nahting.
Only six grade Japanese skool.
Boss say lilamo' English I know wuz
General Foreman can be.

As why you gotta work hod
bumbye boss no like.
You finish skool,
find goood work.

Significant Moments in da Life of Oriental Faddah and Son: COLLEGE

Aftah I wen graduate high school
my Oriental Faddah
wanted me
for go
Harvard, Princeton, Stanford,
AND Yale.

He nevah know
wea any of those places wuz,
jus dat das wea I had fo' go.
So I went
UC Irvine.

Das wea I wen discover
dat my Oriental Faddah
wuzn't really
my Oriental Faddah.

He wuz my
"Asian American" Faddah.

Dey sed I can have one Oriental rug
or some Oriental furnitures,
but I cannot
CAN
NOT
have
one Oriental Faddah.

Oriental is one term you use
for da kine inanimate objecks.

Das wot dey toll me.

So, I toll 'em,
"Oh, my Oriental Faddah,
he hardly sez anyting.
Das kinda like being
one inanimate objeck, ah.
Wotchoo tink?"

Ho, when I sed dat
their faces wen jus
freeeeeze,
like dey couldn't believe
I sed someting
as disrespeckful as dat.

Tsk, "Asian American" das why.

Diff'rent Stations

Da people in my Asian American
Studies class
wuz all grumbling
how when dey wuz growing up
nevah get "Asian American"
role models.
Da only ones dey remembah
is Bruce Lee cuz EVERYBODY knows Bruce,
Arnold from *Happy Days*,
and Kwai Chang Caine
who wuzn't even Chinese,
but das how desperate dey wuz.

I toll 'em brah,
wotchoo talking?
In Hawai'i
had planny shows
wit Oriental peoples.
And dey wen jus look at me
like well, go name some den.

Had *Kikaida*, *Kikaida 0-1*,
Akumaiza 3, *Kamen Rider V-3*
5 Rangers, *JAKQ*, *Battle Fever J*
Rainbow Man, *Condorman*, *Inazuman*
Diamond Eye, *Denjin Zaiboga*, *Robocon*
and *Ikyu-San*
which wuz dat boring cartoon
wit da little bolo-head Japanese boy
who wuz studying for be
one monk
and he always put spit

on top his fingers
den rubbed 'em
on his forehead,
tok tok tok tok,
for help him tink.
But I wuzn't sure if we wuz
counting animated cartoon kine,
cuz if we wuz,
had planny mo'
wea dat came from.

And den
had
all da Samurai kine too,
but I nevah watch those
so I no really know.
All I know is on top one show
one of da guys
had like tattoos all ova his body
and whenevah da bad guys saw him
take his arm outta his sleeve
dey would be all like
"Holy s***! Das da guy!,"
whoevah he wuz sup'post to be.

And den,
I tell 'em no even
get me started
on *Black Belt Theater*
wit Da Mastah Killah,
Fu Sheng, da Five Venom guys
and I wuz starting
for go off again
when one of da guys in my class,
da guy wit da old-school

black frame glasses
came real close to my face
and sed in one real high nose kine way
"Why would you consider them to be
POSITIVE role models?
I bet those FOB's can't even speak
good English.
In a way, they're kind of
like you."

Looking at all a dem
look at me,
made me tink about
Rap's Hawaii
All in the Ohana
Andy Bumatai's High School Daze
Frank Delima's Hawaiian Christmas Carol
Sparks
Pidgin to da Max
Pidgin to da Max Hana Hou
Sistarella
and *Rap's Aloha,*
which wuzn't as good as *Rap's Hawaii.*
In fack might've jus been
all da rejeck skits
dat nevah make 'em into da first one
but we nevah care
wuz always cool for see Rap.

Dey only showed those Local shows
like once a year
if
we wuz lucky.
But wuz always one event.

We would always
all get togeddah
laugh at da TV,
laugh at ourselves on top da TV.

So I just smiled
upped my chin at
da guy wit da black frame glasses
and all da oddah people who had
staring problems.
And I toll 'em "Yeah, so wot.
Why, BODDAH YOU?"

Obaban's Hands

I nevah like get
da kine generic
kanji character,
dat kine most guys get
on da back
of their shoulder blades,
"chikara"
fo' show dey strong,
tough,
cuz one tattoo tells one story—
"Oh, I got chikara
cuz I tink I have muscles"
is kinda one junk story.

My friend Jay
agreed dat cliché kine is junk.
Das da reason why
he nevah like get
one crane, tiger, or dragon.
He sed, Asian American males
are always typecast as being
masters of da martial arts.
So for challenge dat notion
he got one peace symbol instead,
not da Chinese calligraphy kine, but
y'know dat upsidedown airplane in da circle,
which wuz pretty ironic to me
cuz Jay had
one black belt
in Tae Kwon Do
and he liked
getting into fights

and beating people up,
so I figgah-ed advertising
he wanted for beef
would be good, no?

My oddah friend Rayceen,
she cannot even handle
peeling da band-aid off her leg
so we wuz surprised
when she got one sexy
geisha girl
on her lower back
as some kine "feminist statement"
against da stereotype
of da "submissive Asian female."
Someting li'dat she sed.
Wuz one interesting idea,
I tot to myself,
but wouldn't dat only work
if you wuz one loudmout tita girl.
Oddahwise guys going tink
you same same like da picture.
Plus not like those chopsticks
in your hair helps.

For explore my
various tattoo possibilites
I called up my Grandma and axed her
if we had one family crest
and if so
wot da ting looked like?

My Grandma laughed when I axed her.
"Okinawa mostly all farmer, y'know?
Fancy design, das Naichi style,

himakamaka.
Some Okinawa get da mon,
but da design
das all copy
from da Japanee one.
Us, we Uchinānchu. Dey used to
tease us befo' time.
We all da buta kaukau people,
da people who eat pig.
To us, 'ono was. We like pig,
but to dem
pig feet soup
low class food dat was."

I wuz tinking about if
anybody in our family had
any tattoos
and das when I remembered
Obaban.

When I wuz small I wuz sked
for let Obaban
touch me cuz I thought
she had one disease
or someting cuz
da back of her hands
wuz all tattooed,
colored with shapes
of solid black,
like square bruises.

I axed my Grandma
if she knew da meanings for dat.
She sed someting about how
in ancient times

da Uchinānchu high priestess
wuz returning home to Okinawa,
but her boat got lost
in one typhoon
so she ended up in Japan.
Da Japanese lord dude
thought she wuz one hottie
so he kept her prisoner, li'dat.
But da high priestess
wuzn't all looks and no brains.
Witout his knowing
she wen go tattoo
da back of her hands,
so he wouldn't tink
she wuz so pretty anymore.
When da lord dude saw wot she did
he wen freak,
like wot da heck is dat,
so he sent her back home.
And from dat point on,
all da women in Okinawa
started doing 'em
for ward off all da Japanese pirates.
At least das how da legend goes.

Dis made me retink
my whole tattoo theories.
If Okinawa farmer people style
is make yourself look
unattractive as possible
den I no like pay money
for make myself look ugly!

Das when I got da perfeck idea.
When people ax if I evah thought about

getting one tattoo,
I can tell 'em,
Oh, in Okinawa
wuz traditionally
da women who got tattoo-ed
and from dea I can buss out
da story about da whole pirate deals.
Bu-ya. Save money
and
I get one story for tell.

Hajichi: Tattoos and Diamonds is Forevah

I cannot tell
if her hands shaking
cuz she nervous
dat going hurt
or if it's cuz
of da forbiddeness
of her ack,
dat she's here despite
her fiancé's wishes.

Like us,
her fiancé's one Local
Okinawan too
but he's not down
wit da whole idea.
He said getting da tops
of her hands
tattooed is barbaric,
and he equated da practice
to branding
and treating women
like possessions.
Ironically,
he suggested she
could get one tattoo
of his name
instead.

I come involved
when she calls me up
and asks me if I
know anyting

about hajichi.
I tell her I no tink
it's about da husband
doing 'em to da wife
saying you belong to me,
and I share wit her
da Okinawan myth
my grandma toll me,
da one about da princess
who marked her hands
so dat her pirate capture,
whose personal preference
wuz for hands
sans anykine markings,
would find her repulsive
and set her free.
I tell her
to me, da story's
about how da princess
uses her ingenuity
for defeat one more mighty-er
enemy.

Togeddah we
do sa'more research,
wea we learn right around da turn
of da twentieth century
da Japan government
using military force
invaded
and took control
of independent Okinawa.
As time went on, our ancestors
loss control ova
their government,

their lands,
their culture.

An'den da Japan government
banned
da shaman women of da villages,
who did da hajichi tattoos,
from practicing their artform,
in order for allow for one more
homogeneous culture
and easier assimilation
of Okinawans into Japan.

Some Okinawans believed
dat da hajichi ban
wuz one excuse
for round up and imprison
da Okinawan women elders
and break up
their power.
Yet,
despite da fack
dat their culture wuz one crime
many Okinawan women
still continued for get
their hajichi,
as their act
of
resistance.

As my friend passes da photo
of her great grandma's hajichi
to da tattoo artist.
I tell her she lucky she get
dat photo.

I ask her
one more time if she sure.
If she sure, she sure.
Cuz what if her husband-to-be
calls off da wedding?
I remind her dat both
tattoos and diamonds
is forevah.

She looks at da back
of her hand
as she reminds me
dat even in Okinawa
hardly get any women
wit hajichi anymore.
So even though her fiancé
might not like how it looks,
it doesn't matter
what he thinks,
because to her
it's
beautiful,
it's very beautiful.

I note da steadiness,
in her hand,
as she extends her arm
and flips her wrist
so dat da top of her hand
faces outward.

I note da steadiness
in her voice
when she declares,
"If he

don't like it,
he
can talk
to da hand."

Palms Face Up

I ask my Grandma hakum
in every family picture
Obaban stay sitting down
with her hands on her lap
wit her palms face up.

Grandma sez
when Obaban came Hawaiʻi
she wuz shame
cuz none of da oddah women
had dat kine
Okinawan tattoos
on da backs of their hands.
Das why whenevah she went out
no mattah how hot,
she always
wore gloves.

Obaban even toll Grandma
dat when she she ma-ke time
make shua her hands
get da glove on
when she stay in da casket.
Grandma sez
Obaban made her promise.

I ask Grandma
if Obaban wen stay in Okinawa
den would she have been
not shame?

Obaban wuz probably
embarassed
before she came wuz,
Grandma tells.
Because back in Okinawa
everyting Okinawa
wuz coming shame.

Grandma tells me
she heard stories
dat in da schools ova dea
if dey caught you speaking
Uchināguchi
you had for wear
da hogen fuda sign
around your neck
as your punishment
marking da fack
da way you spoke
wuz inferior.

I still no get it.
How can? I ask.
How can be shame Okinawa
when you
IN
Okinawa?

"When Japan took over
Okinawa
dey teach
Okinawa way
not da right way.
Dey teach,
you gotta be like

da mainland."

"Like da 'mainland,'"
I repeat.
And das when
all of a sudden
I can relate li'dat,
you know da kine.

All Mix Up

At UC Irvine
I took Japanese
only cuz everybody
in my family
sed good. Mo bettah fo' me
if in case I like get job
cuz all da tourists in Hawai'i.

And plus
all my friends sed
going going,
come in handy.
I can translate for dem
all da newest Japanese
Gundam animations;
no need wait for
junk English dubbed version.

BUT HO!
Frickin' hod wuz, Japanese.
Da kooky verb ting
change depending
on who you talk to—
if dey mo' up than you
den gotta be polite,
if same same
den das one noddah form,
and if lower than you
den I guess ees okay
to be RUDE.

So I ended up calling
my Grandma planny times
long distance
for help wit da homeworks.
She nevah mind me
calling da house
early in da morning
before my class started
cuz she always got up
5:00 anyway
for water da yard
and listen,
half-awake kine
to da Japanese
radio station.

In fack,
I tink she liked
me calling her planny
cuz when Grandpa wen move out
she nevah have nobody for talk to.
My faddah mostly working
And only me call.
Nobody go visit.

I figured
wit my Grandma's help
I would ace dat class.
Cuz my Grandma wuz at least
twice as old
as my Japanese teachah
who wuzn't even Japanese.
I tink he wuz Korean.

But I dunno wot wen happen.
I wuz getting all my answers
WRONG, brah.
Finally, one day aftah class,
I wen tell da teachah
"Eh, you sure you know
wotchoo talking?
My grandma wen help me, y'know."

He tilted his head at me
den tilted 'em back da oddah way
den thought for two seconds
before he sed "Must be
your Grandmother doesn't speak
proper Japanese.
Perhaps it's
rural Japanese
or provincial."
Den he axed wot part of
Japan she wuz from.

Frickin' A!!!
Finally somebody ask,
"Wot village I from?"
I tried for commit
dat li'lo bit of informations
to permanent memory
but I guess
no mo' such ting as
permanent memory,
cuz I searched
and I searched
my head,
but I couldn't remembah.
So I jus looked at him like

I dunno wotchoo talking 'bout,
shrugged my shoulders,
and walked away.

My grade wuzn't doing
so good
so I called my Grandma
less and less
but I tink she missed
me calling cuz aftah awhile
she
would call
me
for see if I needed help
wit anyting. She even
volunteered for ask
some of Grandpa's old
friends who knew more than her kine.
But I wuzn't taking no chances
on people witout PhD's
like Miyashiro man
or Karate man
or Ten Cen who got his name
cuz he nevah used to have more
than 10 cents to his name,
but dat wuz back in da day
so today his name probably
would be Dollah.

Latah on
when I came back on break
my Grandma wanted for know
wot I got in Japanese.
I toll her da report card
nevah come yet.

And jus so happen
she had da guy,
Ten Cen on da phone
so she toll me go talk to him.
But wot I wuz going say?
I nevah like tell 'em
I wuz tinking of quitting Japanese
when I nevah even tell my Grandma yet.

So I wuz all like
"Eh, Mister Ten Cen. . ."
Ho, I almost called him Mister Dollah.
I toll 'em yeah, my Grandma
wen help me planny, but
I got 'em all WRONG everytime
Mister Ten Cen wen laugh.
Den he wen tell me
"Da way you Grandma talk
to yo' Grandpa. As not
Japanee—Dat one
CHANPURŪ UCHINĀGUCHI!"

"Wot dat?," I wen tell
"Championship Okinawan?"

"No. Wot kine atama you get, boy?"

I could almost feel him
slap my head ova da phone.

"Chanpurū, das ono kine
Okinawan stir-fry kaukau.
Chanpurū Uchināguchi mean
Okinawan,
Japanese,

Hawaiian,
English,
Pidgin,
all mix up
togeddah in one.
Ony in Hawaii, you know
get Chanpurū Uchināguchi."

Only in Hawai‘i,
I repeated insai my head.
Only in Hawai‘i.
Ho, I guess I know
little bit of someting
not too many people know, brah.
Gotta be proud for be
CHIBURU!

Brainstorm: How Fo' Be Mo' Okinawan

1) Start off simple. Buy one cookbook. But, make shua da ting wuz put togeddah by Hui O Laulima or one noddah authentic Okinawan organization das officially recognize by da HUOA, da Hawai'i United Okinawa Association. Dis going enable me for prepare actual Okinawan dishes in da traditional Okinawan manner. Even if da food no taste so garans to me, gotta at least know da theories of wot I "suppost to like" to eat.

2) Magical transference. When get time, cruise wit da old Okinawan people down at Lanakila Center. Maybe I can pick up some Okinawan words or someting. I figgah, if I cruise wit dem long enough, some gotta rub off on me. Somehow, I dunno how; ass why ees called magical transference. But I dunno if can, cuz I work everyday like everybody else. Yeah, who get time cruise wit old people?

3) Learn how fo' do someting. Learn Okinawan dance or learn how for play some kine instrument. Dis one hard but, cuz require skill, li'dat. Too bad I wuzn't in band. I remembah when I wuz small Grandpa wen try teach me sanshin. But he gave up cuz he sed, "You samisen no mo' rhythm." So, for get 'em back, I toll 'em, "Not like you can sing good. Sound like you get all kine mucus," but den I found out das how 'post to be, da song supposed to sound like gala gala.

4) Be hardcore. Make da official pilgrimage and visit da homeland. Everybody go when dey retire. Full-on immersion muss work, no? Cuz dey all claim dey come back feeling mysteriously somehow "more Okinawan." Dey swear dey can feel da connection like ees their version of Mecca. Try call up Uncle Mac today and book one reservation on top one of his tours. Wait, find out how much cost first. Like guys my age get extra money for travel. Maybe das why only old guys go.

5) Da most practical way. Be like everybody else. Jus be Okinawan once-a-year and go Kapiʻolani Park, Okinawan Festival, eat pig feet soup and andāgī. And if I feel like some Okinawan/American fusion cuisine den go grine da combination andāgī/hotdog, oddahwise known as da onolicious "Andadog." And most importantly, cannot forget for buy one Okinawan Festival t-shirt even if da design all kalakoa no match, frickin' purple, yellow, green, red. Gotta get da shirt jus so I can say I went and I get some Uchinānchu pride.

Kaimukī Grandma on Being Uchinānchu

Grandma asks
us grandchildren
if we can tell da difference
between Okinawan
and Naichi.

My cousin jokes
if da last name no sound regulars
and sounds like one made up Japanee name,
like half da names in Rap Reiplinger's
"Japanese Roll Call" skit,
den das gotta be Okinawan.

Disappointed, Grandma scolds her,
"No say dat youuuuu."

Grandma sez
before time in Hawai'i
Naichi nevah like da Okinawans.
She sez da Naichi even made up stories
dat Okinawans wuz more closely related
to monkeys
so das why we wuz darker
and had so much hair.

When Grandma wuz small
she sez one Naichi girl made her cry
cuz she kept telling Grandma
for show her her tail.
Da Naichi girl insisted
all monkeys must have tails.

Okinawans and Naichi diff'rent.
Even till today,
hod for get along,
Grandma lectures us.
As proof she tells us
about when she wen go visit
her Naichi friend
from Kāhala side
who nevah ax her fo' go in da house.
"No mo' da hospitality.
Naichi style dat kine."

Maybe dey nevah invite you in
cuz their house wuz messy, I challenge.
And I ask Grandma if she called before going.

"Das Naichi style," she maintains.

It's not until
months later when Grandma
stay cleaning out her icebox
and get all da freezer food
all ovah da place and unexpecked kine
Miyashiro man comes by for visit
dat Grandma retinks her
original tinkings.

"Me, first time
no mo' nahting,
nahting for serve.
Not even da cold drinks.
Maybe talphone first good idea, no?"

Kaimukī Grandma's Newly Discovered Supah Market Trick

My Grandma always had
one personal preference
for da old Okinawan ways.
But as she gets older
I notice she coming
little bit more open minded.

Da two of us stay Times Supah Market
so I ax her
"Eh, Grandma,
hakum you shakin' da lettuce?"

I tink maybe if da leaf fall off
den das da test,
das means das some pretty junk lettuce
no choose dat one.

But she sez she jus seen
one old Chinese Pākē lady doing dat
da oddah week
so she started for copy.

I ax, "Oh hakum? Wot's da purpose?"

She sez da Chinese lady wen explain,
"You do dat
for take off
da extra waddah,
scale come mo' light."
Shinbōnin.
Save money.
Good idea I tink so.

Da Art of Eating

Unlike da haole people on TV
who practice please pass da potatoes,
my Grandpa had his own kine etiquette.
"Suck 'em up"
is da expression
some guys my Oriental Faddah's age use.
Usually dat wuz fo' drinks
but my Grandpa wen apply 'em to food.
Ho, whenevah he ate
saimin, pig feet soup, or even fish
he always made dat slurping noise.
He would slurp his noodles
snort his soup
syphon all da meat off da fish bones
and den suck out da eye.
I always tot dat wuz rude
but my Grandpa sed das how.
Someting about
gotta make plenny noise
so make da cook feel good
and let 'em know
dat da food taste ono.

People always axing me
how's my Grandpa.
I hate when dey ax.
I dunno wot fo' say.
So I jus say, "He's okay.
Still da same.
Still at Maunalani."
Pretty nice up dea.
Unreal da view.

Can jus kickback
and look at Diamond Head.
So quiet I can hear
da nurses talking story in da hall,
da finches cruising by da patio window,
da crazy old lady singing
"Manuela Boy" next door,
but I cannot hear
my Grandpa
eating his food
from da tube.

No Escape

We sign in.
We see him during
visiting hours
and only during
special visiting hours
because
according to da warden
"Those are
the rules."

Everyday dey feed him
da same banana mush
and if he no ack up,
dey give 'em small cup water.
Can tell from his face,
I know he like break out
so he can go grab
one massive plate lunch
from Masu's.

I know he raddah play Paiyut
wit da boys down on River Street.
He no like
watch old Gene Kelly movies,
sing "You Are My Sunshine,"
and toss around da beach ball
with all da oddah inmates.

I like believe
da criminal mind
of da notorious
River Street Gambler

get 'em all thought out.
I like believe
he just playing along
biding his time
playing stupid games,
waiting for da right moment
for put his plan into action
and make
da perfeck getaway.

But sometimes
ees da little tings
dat can go wrong.
Early dis morning
during da middle of da night
da nurse on duty caught him
trapped hanging
over his bed,
on top da safety rail.

But maybe wuz for da bettah,
cuz I no tink he would've made 'em
past da door
wit da fire alarm.

Grandpa's Ancient Medicine

When da jellyfish wen go sting me
  my Grandpa toll me make shi shi on top.
Da times I had stuck doo doo
  he gave me some prune juice fo' drink.
And wheneva I had mosquito bite
  jus spit and put tsuba he sed.
He toll me fo' eat da fish eye
  for bettah vision
  but I nevah like cuz gross, ah.

Whenevah my Grandpa had itchy rash
  he rubbed vinegar.
Da time he wen go cut his leg
  he wen put aloe from da backyard.
Doze days when he had sore throat
  he wen gargle salt water.
And whenevah he burn himself on da stove
  he jus smear on some
  Arm & Hammah Baking Soda.

Doze wuz not bad
  you should see da hardcore kine
  treatments. Unreal.
When he caught one cold
  he wen cure 'em wit his formula—
  twenny year old garlic
  soaked in whisky
  in da brown kim chee jar.
When his body wuz all achin'
  he lit one senkō
  from his bottom dresser drawer
  and did yaito

on da proper pressure point,
burning away da pain.

Now my Grandpa stay hospital—
    Brain Hemorrhage.
Da doctors wen operate
    but dey no tink he goin' be da same.

If he could only eat da fish brain.

I once toll my Grandpa
    he should write down all his recipes
    so he no forget 'em.
He sed, "No can depend book.
In case lose, wot?
Mo' bettah leave in head
    den stay inside
    forevah."

Significant Moments in da Life of Oriental Faddah and Son: MARRIAGE

I came back home
wit one girlfriend
fiancée actually
who wuz one katonk.

Only she nevah know she wuz
one katonk.
She probably mo' used to
da term
banana.

Either way, my Oriental Faddah
wuz happy
katonk, banana,
TWINKIE,
so long as Oriental he sed.

"Asian American," she correck-ed.

Jus for fun
I took her to one
Frank Delima show
at da Polynesian Palace.

But she nevah laugh,
not even one chuckle
for wot she called
"the blatant
stereotyping
and racist
ethnic portrayals."

So I started playing around, brah.
Aftah da show,
I started telling all my friends

"Eh, wassup Oriental!"

"Ooo, you friggin' Oriental!"

"Brah, yo' Mama, she so Oriental
I bet she cannot see her chopsticks
unless she turn 'em sideways!"

I figgah I would take back
da term!

If Popolo people can
use da "N" word, den hakum
I cannot use da one
dat starts wit "O?"

EMPOWERING li'dat.

She tot I wuz nuts.
Out of my freakin' mind!

So she got back on her plane
and leff.

Looking in da air
all I could tink wuz
Wot Lucille,
You going leave me now?!

Even though Lucille
wuzn't even
her name.

Da Box Nobody Could Open

I dunno if your Daddy
tell you dis story, but
I go tell you
so you know.

Grandpa good man you know,
but at first he nevah like
your Daddy.

He wanted your Mama find
strong boy
who can take care her.
He tell your Mama
"You marry dis one polio,
bumbye pohō."

One day Obaban come
all da way country-sai for visit.
Grandpa went out holoholo,
so he nevah see wot happen.

Obaban bring big box,
almost as big as dis stove.

I get two strong sons,
dey can put 'em down from da car,
but two no can open.
Even wit hammer no can.
Kenneth try.
Richard try.

Your daddy see, he go
Grandpa tool house
get diff'rent tool.

He come back
Tok tok.
One time hemo.
No mo' sweat.

Obaban see dat
she grab my arm.
Nodding her head
she tell
"Jinbun ga aru, boy!"
Dis one small, but get brains.

Da Photo Album My Mom Made

She left me,
as one dying away
present,
one cloth-covered photo album,
with my name stitched
on da cover
in cursive letters.

I get up some nights
for look at pictures of
her hands washing me
in da kitchen sink,
her bosom as she cradles me
in her arms, me
all alone,
lying on top
da orange zabuton,
smiley faced and oblivious.

I tink, too bad
as one baby
I nevah have camera too.
I can only imagine
da smile
I brought
to her.

Un-told Stories

One day:

I ax my Grandma for tell me
some stories
about my Mom.

She tells me one
about how high school time
my Mom wanted for learn piano,
but my Grandpa sed no,
no can.
Ony rich people learn dat kine.

So my Grandma wen secret kine
save up on da side
for pay for da lessons.
Every week two times
my Mom used to go aftah school.

Den couple years when she came good
she bought one used piano
from da Salvation Army store
and announced she wuz going start
charging people for lessons.
And people came.

Das when my Grandpa changed his tune
"My daughter piano teachah you know,"
he bragged to his friends
especially Karate Man who always tot
he wuz all dat.

Next day:

I ax my Grandma for tell me
sa' more stories
about my Mom.

I like da one she toll me yestahday.
I vaguely remembah her telling me
dat piano one when I wuz small
so I like for see if get
any oddah ones I kinda sorta remembah too.

But she tells me da piano one again
I guess she forgot she toll 'em to me
jus da oddah day.
But I no interrupt
cuz I no mind hearing 'em again.

But dis time some of da details change
so I ax my Grandma if wuz twice a week
or chree times a week for da lessons.
If da piano wuz from Salvation Army
or from one garage sale?
If wuz Karate Man or Ten Cen
dat Grandpa used to brag to?

Today my Grandma sez she dunno
but da oddah day she sed 'em
wit so much certainty
dat I would nevah question
any of da details.

Maybe tomorrow I'll ax her
for tell 'em to me again,
one mo' time.

Two outta chree?

I Wuz Dea

Nobody really eva toll me
how it all went down.
Wuz kinda like
you wuz dea
you should know
but I wuz too young
for remembah
anyting
hardly.

I check out da State Library
for old newspapah articles
so I can read
for find out exackly
wot wen happen.

Scanning da microfiche
I start for come queasy
little bit.
I dunno if can handle.
I look couple chree times,
but not on da front page
or even in da first section.
I check again for make shua
I get da right date.

Finally I find 'em
da brief mention stay buried,
mixed in wit da traffic report.
One column. Chree short paragraphs.
"Kaimukī Traffic Snarled."
Talks about angry motorists

who wuz late for work.
Stores complaining
about da loss of business.
Nobody wen talk to any of da people
who worked wit my Mom
who went school wit my Mom
who wuz related to my Mom
who knew my Mom at all.
Da only mention of her had
wuz "one fatality."
Nevah even get her name.
Da only reason
I knew wuz her
is cuz
I wuz dea.

How I Post to Know?

Dat Okinawan word
both my parents probably knew
but nevah
evah used.

I remembah
only my
Maui Grandma
used to use 'em,
but I only saw her
when I wuz small
couple few times
every oddah summah.

I remembah
my Maui Grandma
get deaf ear
so wuz only easy
catch her by surprise.
Whenevah I scare her
she would tell,
"AKISAMIYO!"

I remembah
my Maui Grandma
whenevah she found out
someting
dat everybody else but her
knew
she would tell,
"AKISAMIYO!"

Twenny-eight years
aftah da fack
I try ask my Maui Grandma
for teach me
some Okinawan words
so I start by asking her
for tell me
wot
"aki-
sami-
YO"
means.

Maui Grandma's head
jerks back
and she yells,
"Akisamiyo,
hakum you
dunno
Akisamiyo?!
Akisamiyo. . .
'Oh my goodness.'"

Akisamiyo indeed.

Naming one Okinawan Baby

When my Grandma hears
wot my cousin
going name her baby
she tells ME
she
no like
da name.

Grandma
tells me,
not MY COUSIN mind you,
dat da name Maya
is like da Okinawan saying
Gachi Mayā.

I ask my Grandma wot das means.

She says before time
she would see
my little cousin eat
planny chocolate candy
so she'd shake her head
and tell
Gachi Mayā,
likening my cousin
to one greedy cat.

She says she worries dat
gachi Maya child
come gluttonous for candy
den gluttonous for food
and bumbye come

gluttonous for everyting.

I laugh
cuz my cousin,
da stock broker
wit her Lexus SUV and LV bag,
can be known for appreciate
da finer tings in life,
so I see her choosing dat name
as little bit ironic.

My cousin,
who's half Okinawan by da way,
is so proud
of her name choice
cuz she looked up da Greek meaning,
da Hindu meaning,
da Hebrew meaing,
and she says she even found
one meaning in Japanese.

My Grandma sez I shouldn't
say anyting to my cousin.
But I wondah if my Grandma really
no like me say anyting
den fo' why she telling me someting.

In da end I jus remind my cousin
dat good she found
one Japanese meaning
cuz she is half Japanese.
But I kinda trow da hint
and I ask her if she knows
da Okinawan meaning too.

Okinawan Proverb

Okinawa means "rope in the open sea."

When my Great Grandparents came Hawai'i
all dey knew wuz Uchināguchi.

Some Okinawan trickled down to
my Grandparents
and even less
to my parents.
Hardly anyting
wuz passed
down
to
me.

All the Ryūkyū islands put toggedah
is said for resemble one long rope in da ocean.

In my research of old
Okinawan proverbs
I come across one
dat sez

*Nmarijima nu kutuba wasshī nē
kuni n wasshīn.*

If you forget your native tongue,
das means your forget your native country.

If all da people maintain their grip on da rope
den da connection between those people going stay strong.

Aftah reading dat I come gung ho
for visit da homeland
I nevah knew,
but when I talk story
wit my Uncle Mac
who goes Okinawa planny
he sez each trip
he sees less and less
old people
and he hears
less and less
Uchināguchi.
He sez Okinawan
no mo' any cachet;
most young people
jus no see
any use
in learning 'em.

Once everyone le-la goes da rope
da rope falls into da ocean and becomes lost at sea.

Da Fort Street Musician

I knew someting wuz up
cuz people no usually gather 'round
listen to da weirdos.

Typically dey stay
real far away
from da guys who go on and on
about
da upcoming social
or spiritual
revolution.

People downtown too busy—
dey gotta
close deals,
open new doors,
climb ladders,
jump through hoops,
cuz da only place dey like
STAY
is ahead,
but you can't do dat
when you take a break
and stop, jus to listen
to some weirdo
preaching on top da sidewalk
by Fort Street Mall.

I nevah like make
monkey see, monkey do
so I wuzn't going try look,
but I could hear

wot sounded like music,
kinda jazzy, kinda Hawaiian, but yet
kinda reminded me of da kine
old Okinawan songs my Grandpa used to sing.

So I wuz all shock
when I made my way through da crowd
and I seen
one young Okinawan-looking guy,
around twenty-five years old
wit his eyes closed,
playing da strings on his
snake-skin sanshin
jus like how my Grandpa used to do.
His voice drawing out each
Okinawan syllable,
like he
wuz one old man
who had all da time in da world
for finish dat song.

I tried for find his hat,
so I could trow in my dollah and dig,
cuz I tot all street musicians
get one hat,
but I looked
and I couldn't find.
Instead, aftah his performance
he busted out for sale
some of his CDs.

Planny guys leff
but some of us stayed
and formed one line, wit me
being da very last guy.

I looked at my watch cuz
I had to head back, go work.
But da line wuz moving slow,
cuz da guy, Norman,
wuz talking story little bit
wit everybody—
da businessman in his spiffy suit,
da foreign exchange student,
and even dat bummy-guy
who smelled like he nevah bocha
in days.

I wuz tinking, ho,
how dis guy Norman came so good?
Most guys his age play
electric guitar or 'ukulele.
I remembah when I wuz small
my Grandma sed I should learn
Okinawan dance.
But I sed "Das for GIRLS!"
She sed get boy kine too.
I sed I nevah like, so my Grandpa
wanted for teach me
sanshin, but I sed to him "Nah,
cannot even understand da words;
no sound like singing,
sound like you gargling your Listerine."
My Grandma toll him "Go teach, go teach."
But my Grandpa sed "Ahhhh, him waste time.
Pohö teach if he no like learn."

I got to da front
and Norman wuz starting for pack up
his briefcase;
he sed he had to go to his job

pretty soon,
but he made small kine
conversations wit me.
He axed if I wuz Okinawan
and wot my name wuz.
I toll 'em. But he sed,
"No, what's your LAST name?"

Aftah I paid for my CD,
he wanted for know if I played
any Okinawan music too.
I shook my head,
den he sed all joking kine,
"Eh, wot kine Okinawan you?"
I looked at him
den I looked at me
and I toll 'em,
"I dunno,"
and I shrugged my shoulders.

He shook my hand and sed
"Nice meeting you,"
so I toll 'em "K-dens,"
and I watched him head to
da bus stop on Hotel Street
wit sanshin in hand.

I turned around
and made my way through
da tail end of da lunch crowd
while walking leisurely
in da opposite direction
I read
da back
of his CD

for try see
which song I wuz going
listen to
first.

Chiburu Journal

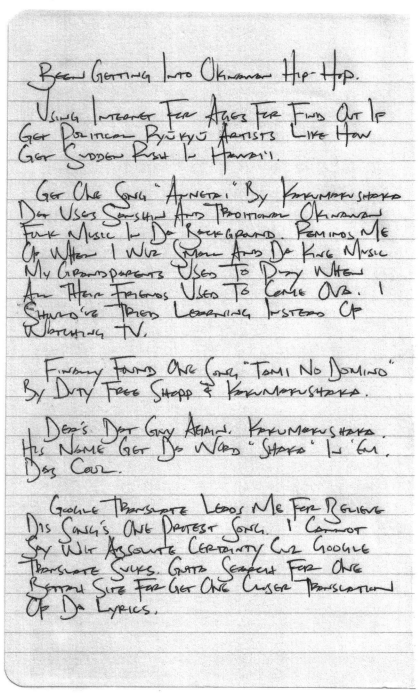

Been getting into Okinawan Hip-Hop.

Using Internet for ages for find out if get political Ryūkyū artists like how get sudden rise in Hawai'i.

Get one song "Ajineri" by Kakumakushaka dat uses Sanshin and Traditional Okinawan Folk Music in da background. Reminds me of when I wuz small and da kine music my grandparents used to play when all their friends used to come ova. I should've tried learning instead of watching TV.

Finally found one song "Tami No Domino" by Duty Free Shopp & Kakumakushaka.

Dea's dat guy again. Kakumakushaka. His name get da word "Shaka" in 'em. Das cool.

Google Translate leads me for believe dis song's one protest song. I cannot say wit absolute certainty cuz Google Translate sucks. Gatta seapch for one bettah site for get one cleaer translation of da lyrics.

Song Talks About Da 2004 US Army Helicopter Crash Into Okinawa International University And Da Anti-American Military Protest Dat Followed.

I Wen Hear About Da 1995 Incident About Da 12-Year Old Okinawan Girl Getting Raped By Da 3 US Servicemen. And Jus Recent Had Da US Marine Wuz Accused Of Raping One 14-Year Old Okinawan Girl, But I Nevah Hear About Dis Helicopter News.

Been Reading A Lot About Okinawa's Histories Wit Japanese Colonialism And American Imperialism, But Get Lotta Current Stuff Going On Dat I Dunno.

I Curious If Get One Okinawan Sovereignty Movement Ova Dea. And If It's Strong Like Da Hawaiian Sovereignty Movement Ova Hea. Get Plenny Yet Dat I Dunno. I Gotta Go Find Out.

Grandma's Question

Eh-rytime I stop by for see
my Grandma
she ax me
da same question.

"Did you go grave?"

I try not for look guilty
when I tell her,
"Grandma,
I raddah spend my time
visiting alive people. . .
Das why I always come visit
you."

"So,"
she tell,
"when I ma-ke,
what?
Pau den,
come see Grandma?"

Grandma's Boxes

Aftah we visit Grandpa in da nursing home, she axes if my
new fiancée owns one pink kerchief. I wanna say, "Nah, keep 'em
Grandma. Can use 'em later." But I hold on to 'em, jus for make her
happy. She wants to give most of her mementos to Big Brothers/Big
Sisters. I wanna tell her, "No Grandma, no give nahting away." I wanna
horde 'em all in one enormous warehouse—somewhere.

I wanna save her expensive yellow and red kimono made from no-can-
     wash bingata material along with da matching hanagasa hat.

I wanna save her frilly pillow with the fifty states and da fifty
     state flowers colorfully hand-embroidered in front.

I wanna save her porcelain sumo wrestler book ends aggressively
     embracing her favorite *Good Housekeeping* magazines.

I wanna save her nori containers filled wit chalky green pennies
     and leftover yen from her and Grandpa's trip to Okinawa ten
     years ago.

I wanna save her 101 different variations of andāgī: chocolate-
     filled, sugar-coated, Mrs. Toguchi's sour cream secret, and
     oddah recipes yet for be invented.

I wanna save her stories of how she and Grandpa struggled to save
     up da $5,000 downpayment to buy their house in Kaimukī and
     worked hard to make da necessary $70 a month mortgage
     payments.

I wanna save her memories of how my mom gave da lei to her favorite
     Japanese singer, Akira Kobayashi, when he came in concert at
     the Nippon Theater and so das how I got my middle name.

I wanna save her anecdotes about how I cried all da way to KEC
    preschool, so she used to walk wit me and wait outsai
    crocheting under da treehouse smiling every time I
    looked out da door for see if she wuz still there.

I wanna save her voice dat softly sang along wit da songs on da
    Japanese radio station.
I wanna save her moments when she jus sat quietly watching *As The
    World Turns*.
I wanna save her silent strength.
I wanna
save
her.

For da Funeral

We look
for one good portrait picture
for da funeral service tomorrow
at Hosoi mortuary.

Me, my Oriental Faddah
and my uncle, aunty guys,
we find planny
old pictures
and nobody knows
if das Grandma when she wuz small,
how dis person stay related to us,
wea dat picture wuz taken at,
or why Grandpa
wuz so dressed up
on one particular day.

I shake my head
cuz dem;
hakum dey nevah ask
when dey had
da chance
for get
da names, dates, places?

Now we stuck
with all these pictures
of faces,
unfamiliar.

Cleansing

I know wot I know
from observation
not cuz he toll me straightforward.

I know
he no even believe
in da kine Chinatown herb doctor
like all da regular ORIENTAL people,
da kine wea get da old guy
who takes out all kine weird stuff
from those little drawers
like Bat's Wing, Snake Skin Powder,
and Dragon's doo doo or wotevahs,
cuz twenty years ago
he tried 'em once when he caught cold
and nevah work so dat wuz da last time
he went ova dea.

And
I know
he no believe
like all da regular people,
in da kine prescription medications,
da kine you get from da real doctor,
cuz he nevah goes for his check-ups
unless he get someting
he deems for be serious
like da time he had
one mild heart attack.

Recently I kinda suprise
when I see

all kine pill bottles
from da Health Food Store
popping up at his house.
And ees strange dat he feels
compelled for explain.
He tells me
"Das all cutting edge stuff.
You gotta be mo' modern
than modern medicine.
Jason Winter's Tea for overall vitality.
Anavit for strengthen da immunity system.
And Brain Gain for enchance
da mind."

He even trying out dat colonic deals
wea you gotta shove dat ting
up your DA KINE.

Dis one I find out when I happen
for walk into da bachroom
while he wuz doing his
cleansing.

I turn around fass kine
cuz bad enough you imagine yourself
doing someting li'dat,
but worse when you actually see someone else
doing it.

Das when all of a sudden
I get one flashback
to one image
from long time ago.
And I dunno wea da memory came from,
wuz like dea

always insai my head,
but packed away
in one little mental storage box
dat my brain forgot about.

Wuz couple weeks aftah
my Mom passed away
and every night I couldn't sleep.
One night I had for wake up
for go make shi-shi.
I walked down da hall
and I heard one noise
coming from bachroom.
Da door wuzn't shut all da way
and through da crack,
I could see da light
from da moon
shining down on da toilet.
He
wuz jus sitting dea
crying
in da dark.

I remembah I wanted for
go in da bachroom
and ask him
hakum he wuz crying.
I wanted for say
someting
like no cry Dad.
I love you.
You know,
someting for make him
feel little bit bettah.

But I nevah.

Instead
I went back
to my room
hid underneath
my blanket
and started crying too.

I hear one flushing.
Das when he comes out carrying
one red hot-water bottle in one hand
and one long tube in da oddah.
When he passes me in da hall
he no say anyting
and I no say nahting back.

For some reason my eyes get teary,
but I suck it up.

Before he walks back
to his bedroom
I ask him
if anyting stay
wrong.

He stops, turns around.
And he tells me.

Significant Moments in da Life of Oriental Faddah and Son: DEATH

Right befo'
my Oriental Faddah died
he suddenly had
planny fo' say.

"No watch *Kingpin*,
da movie juuunk.
The English Patient
mo' bettah wuz, but
not as good as
da book."

Ho, dat shocked da hell outta me.
I nevah know he went movies,
let alone read books.

I tot he jus stayed home
watched *Abarenbo Shogun*
on KIKU
and drank da kine green tea, li'dat.

But now he
wuz giving me
da lowdown
on all da latest movies.

I toll 'em, aw
I could jus picture him
on TV, brah.
At The Movies
wit Roger Ebert

and my Oriental Faddah.
And people would still ax, ah?
"Oh, which one is Ebert?"
DUH, like, da one das NOT Oriental!

He laughed little bit
den he coughed
and axed
real soft
if I tot people
would really mix up
him
and Roger Ebert.

I toll 'em
Nah,
Roger Ebert
get glasses.

Das wot I toll
to
My FADDAH.

Much Mahalos

Shout out to Maui Grandma and Kaimukī Grandma who raised me for be guuru boy, nee. Miss u Mom. Tank you planny to my Grandpas, Aunty Jane, and of course no can forget my one and only Faddah.

Lotsa luv to my dayshift supahvisah Leicie and my nightshift supahvisah Tracie, cuz you guys treat me awesome.

Much mahalos to Write Club. I know I breaking da first rule of Write Club, but I really like talk about Write Club. To all my friends from my writing groups—Carrie Takahata, Normie Salvador, Lisa Kanae, Kimo Armitage, Michael Puleloa, Kyle Koza, Noelle Kahanu, and Hina Kahanu—you guys is da besses.

Supa shaka to Buddy Bess. You believed when nobody else would!

An'den I like give one shout out to all da people who wen help me out wit dis collection along da way. To Da "OG" Eric Chock, Kent "Yoda" Sakoda, Uncle Mac Yonamine, Grant "Sandaa" Murata, Shari Tamashiro and da LIVEyuimaaru committee, Norman Kaneshiro, Jon Itomura, David Miyashiro, Jimmy Toyama, Christy Takamune and da JCCH, Leonore Higa, Rob "Mister" Wilson, Micheline Soong, John Kearns, and all da editors who previously published some of da poems befo', I give you all my appreciations.

Lastly, I like give my gratitude to da mean lady who pushed me and toll me I should write about dis kine personal stuffs. Hea it is. So wot, you going be nice to me now?